The Story of the First Vision

First Edition

FoxCoveBooks

Printed in the United States

The Story of the

FIRST VISION

Written by David Pace
Illustrated by Alycia Pace

When he was young, Joseph Smith lived in a town where there were lots of churches.

He was confused

because all of the churches

taught different things.

He studied and studied to figure out which church was the right one.

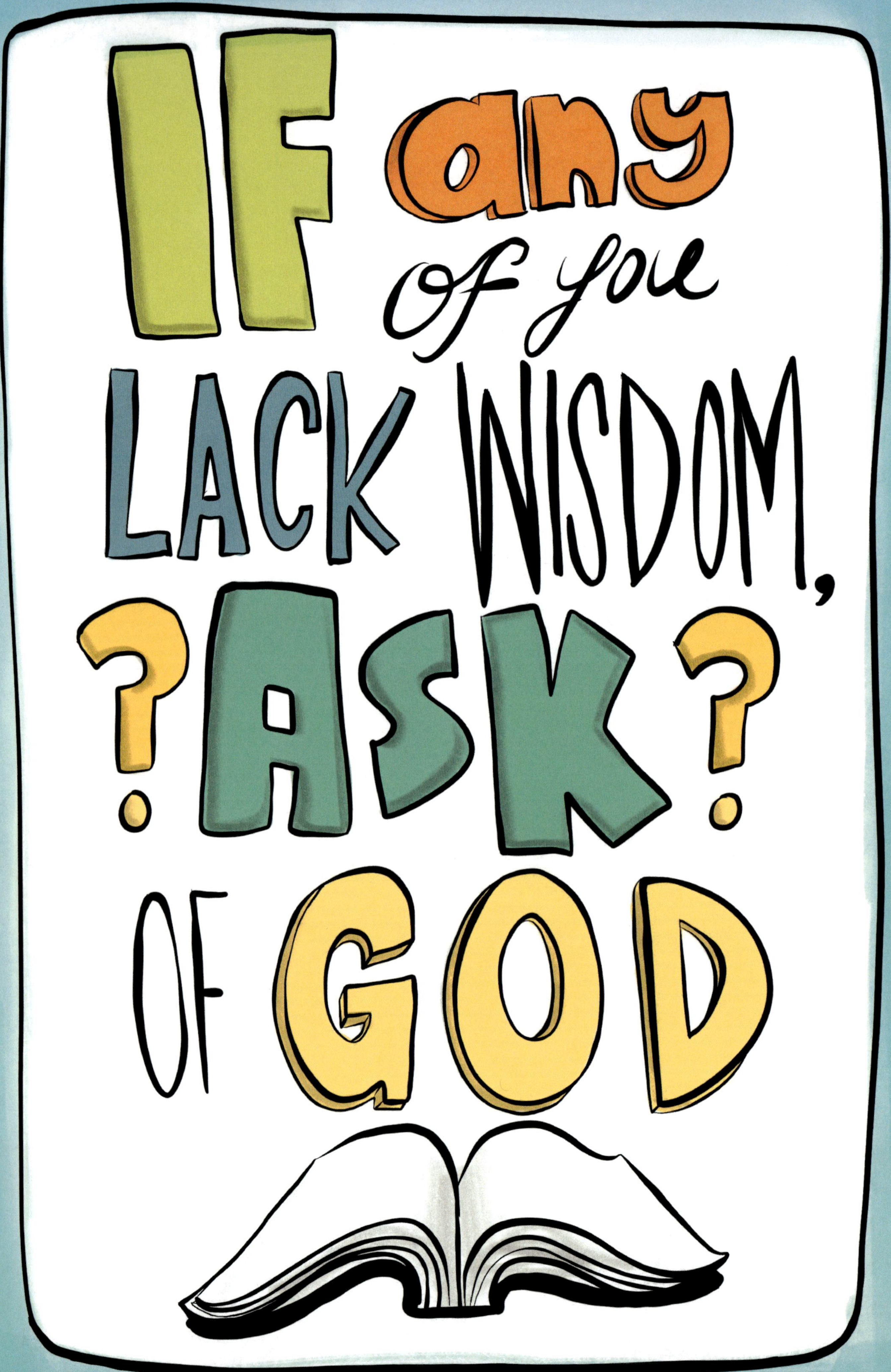
IF any
of you
LACK WISDOM,
?ASK?
OF GOD

James 1:5 prompted Joseph to pray to know which church was correct.

When he was just 14 years old, he went into a grove of trees near his home to pray and ask God which church he should join.

He knelt down and began to pray.

In his words this is what happened next:

"I saw a pillar of light exactly over my head, above the brightness of the sun, which descended gradually until it fell upon me.....When the light rested upon me I saw two Personages, whose brightness and glory defy all description, standing above me in the air. One of them spake unto me, calling me by name and said, pointing to the other -- This is My Beloved Son. Hear Him!"

-Joseph Smith History 1:16-17

Those personages were God
and Jesus Christ.

They explained to Joseph that none of the churches were true and that he should join none of them.

Joseph was then led by God to establish Christ's church on the earth. The church of Jesus Christ of Latter-day Saints.

Check out more of our books at:
www.foxcovebooks.com

Follow us on instagram at:
foxcovebooks

Made in the USA
San Bernardino, CA
26 February 2020